*For my Mom and Dad,*
*who have shown me how to love volcanoes, earthquakes,*
*and the rest of God's Creation.*

Chariot Books is an imprint of ChariotVictor Publishing
Cook Communications, Colorado Springs, CO 80918
Cook Communications, Paris, Ontario
Kingsway Communications, Eastbourne, England

VOLCANOES AND EARTHQUAKES
© 1997 by Michael Carroll

ISBN 1-56476-602-0
Design: Andrea Boven
First printing, 1997
Printed in the United States
01 00 99 98 97     5 4 3 2

Paintings by Michael Carroll
Photo Copyright Credits:
p. 9, 30 Geyser (Michael Carroll)
p. 9 Mount Saint Helens before and after (U.S. Geological Survey)
p. 9 Lava Flows (Michael Carroll)
p. 10 Thera (Charles Pellegrino)
p. 12 Sinai Peninsula (NASA/JSC)
p. 12 Mountains of Northern California (Denis Patrick)
p. 14,31 Mount Ararat (John Morris, Institute for Creation Research)
p. 14 Mount Jabal Al Lawz (Bob Cornuke)
p. 16 Folded Rocks/Bryce Canyon (Michael Carroll)
p. 18 Canaan (Duane Cory)
p. 21 Blue Icebergs, Bering Glacier, Crevasse in glacier (Michael Carroll)
p. 21 Iceberg (Laurie Berg)
p. 22,30 Craters (Michael Carroll)
p. 24 Moab, Arches, Goblin Valley (Michael Carroll)
p. 25 Thingvullir (Michael Carroll)
p. 27 Kobe, Japan (Hosaka/GAMMA)
p. 28 Ganymede inset (NASA/JPL)

# VOLCANOES AND
# EARTHQUAKES

# INTRODUCTION

*. . . since the creation of the world God's invisible qualities—his eternal power and divine nature—have been clearly seen . . . from what has been made.* Romans 1:20

Ever since God spoke the universe into being, our Earth has been changed and shaped by many powerful things. Volcanoes spew rocks and smoke into the sky. Earthquakes shake the land and thrust mountains up, changing the look of the landscape. Glaciers slowly move down mountains, digging out valleys in the rock. We see God's power when we look at His creation beneath our feet, deep inside the Earth.

We are about to go on an adventure to high mountains, thundering volcanoes, wonderful floating mounds of ice, and deep canyons. We will see the places where Moses and Noah walked, and discover the secret places within the Earth that they never saw. And when we see these places, and look at the powers at work inside the Earth, we will see how and why the world got to be the way it is today. And most important, we will see the power and majesty of God in His creation.

**Our world has many wonderful places which have been shaped by forces deep inside the Earth and forces from above.**

# VOLCANOES AND GEYSERS

**The heat from within the Earth drives volcanoes and geysers.**

*You came near and stood at the foot of the mountain while it blazed with fire to the very heavens, with black clouds and deep darkness.*
Deuteronomy 4:11

Deep inside the Earth, the rocks are so hot that they melt. Melted rock is called *magma,* and magma is HOT! The rocks inside the Earth get hot because of two things: heat left over from the creation, and something called *radioactivity.*

Rocks made of unstable atoms are called *radioactive* rocks. They give off energy of their own that is different from the heat given off by other rocks. All of this heat and radioactivity trapped inside the Earth has to come out somewhere, and it does. It comes out of the ground in the form of *volcanoes* or *geysers.*

Volcanoes are holes or cracks in the Earth's surface where hot magma, fire, and smoke blow out into the air. So much liquid rock and ash comes out of the holes that it builds up into a giant mountain! Sometimes, older volcanoes that have already become mountains blow off part of their mountaintop! This happened to a mountain called Mount Saint Helens in Washington State. The explosion of this volcano threw tons of rock and steam high into the sky and flattened whole forests as if the trees were little toothpicks. The ash from Mount Saint Helens turned a beautiful wilderness area into a moonscape.

Not all of the Earth's inner heat escapes as lava or smoke. Sometimes magma touches lakes of water that are buried deep underground. When this happens, hot water and steam shoots out of the ground in a bubbling burst called a geyser. Geysers are found all over the world, but some of the most famous are in America's Yellowstone National Park. Here geysers and steaming ponds stain the landscape in beautiful colors, and huge, multicolored mud puddles bubble up like giant bowls of soup!

In Iceland, there is a geyser for which all geysers are named. Here we see boiling water erupting from *Geysir* while people watch.

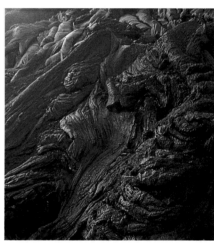

*Inset, top and middle* Mount Saint Helens, a volcano in Washington state, exploded with such force that the entire top blew off, flattening forests and causing an ash "snowfall" for hundreds of miles around.

*Inset, bottom* Many types of lava come from a volcano. This picture shows *pahoehoe*, named after the Hawaiian word for "rope".

Parts of the Minoan town on Thera have been buried under tons of volcanic dust. Here, part of the city has been dug up.

# Volcanoes under the Sea

*Top* **The island of Surtsey is the tip of a volcano that came out of the ocean near Iceland.**

*Bottom* **There are many volcanoes in many places, even on the ocean floor.**

We cannot see some of the Earth's volcanoes, because they are under water! As you read this, many volcanoes are spewing out lava and rocks deep under the ocean. Sometimes a volcano grows big enough that it rises out of the water, forming an island. The Hawaiian islands are all old volcanoes. New volcanoes are still erupting on the biggest island, called Hawaii.

In ancient times, like today, volcanoes out in the ocean or on land buried entire cities or even kingdoms. One such place was the island volcano of Thera. Thera was once the home of a powerful group of people called the Minoans. The Minoans were great artists and sailors. People all over the ancient world knew them. Then suddenly, buildings fell in earthquakes, clouds of poisonous smoke came down the mountain, and the ocean around Thera boiled. The island of Thera exploded and sank into the sea. Most people seem to have escaped before it happened. Today we can find the ancient cities of Thera buried beneath the volcanic stone, or lava, of what is left of this beautiful Mediterranean island.

Off the coast of Iceland, scientists actually saw an island being born. The birthday of the island called Surtsey was on November 17, 1963. The ocean began to boil, and smoke and ash thundered out of the sea. Soon a cone of hot rock appeared, with smoke billowing from its center. Today, the island of Surtsey is a wildlife preserve. It is a very dangerous place because sometimes lava and smoke still pour out from deep within it.

*Left* **Over a thousand years before the time of Christ, the Minoan civilization was destroyed when the island of Thera, its capital, exploded in a volcanic eruption. Tidal waves wiped out many coastal towns.**

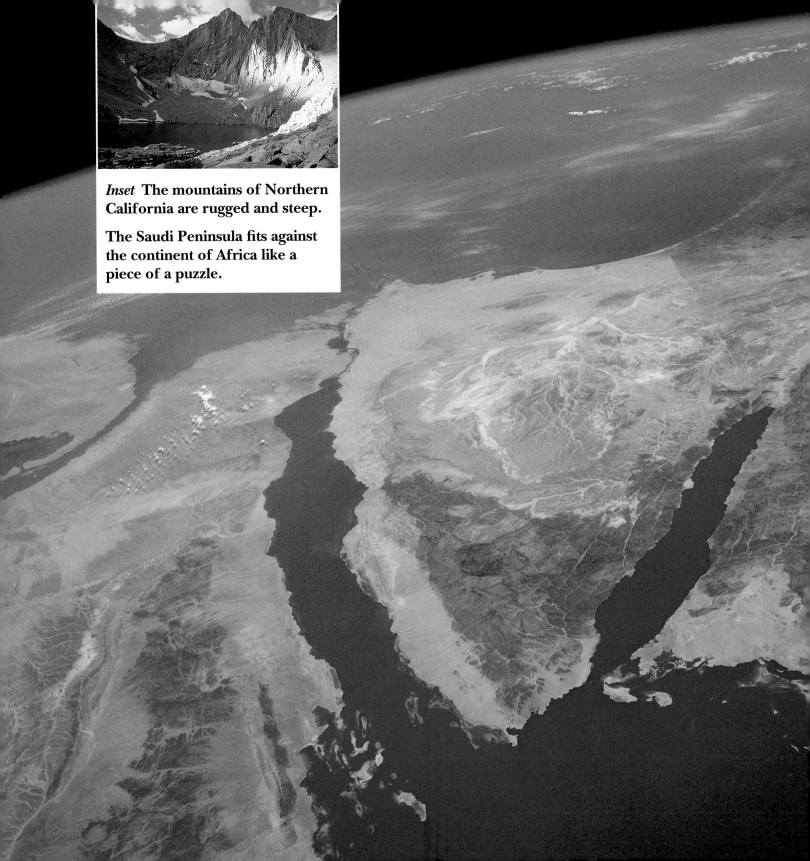

*Inset* The mountains of Northern California are rugged and steep.

The Saudi Peninsula fits against the continent of Africa like a piece of a puzzle.

# MOUNTAINS

*He who forms the mountains, creates the wind, and reveals his thoughts to man . . . the LORD God Almighty is his name.* Amos 4:13

**The ruins of a Tibetan monastery sit at the foot of Mount Everest, the highest mountain in the world.**

Mountains are the highest places on Earth. They usually have steep sides, and their tops can be very sharp and rocky. The top of a mountain is called a *peak*. Many mountain peaks are covered in snow all year, because high places are cold and the snow never melts.

Mountains come in groups, called *ranges*. The highest mountains are in the mountain range called the Himalayas in Asia. Mountain ranges wander across every continent. Some are young, while others are old. The older mountains are smooth with rounded peaks. The younger mountains are sharper on top.

Mountains are made in several ways. As we have seen, some mountains are volcanoes. They build themselves up by pouring lava and ash out of the ground. Other mountains are shoved up by the Earth itself. The Earth's crust is made like a giant puzzle. Its puzzle pieces, called *plates,* float on magma. When two pieces bump into each other, they push up mountains.

The tallest mountain in the world is called Mount Everest. It rises nearly five and one-half miles above sea level. It looks like a beautiful, black pyramid with snow on it. The air is so thin on Everest's high peak that most climbers bring bottles of oxygen to breathe. The Matterhorn in Switzerland is one of the most famous mountains in Europe. Mount Fujiyama is a beautiful volcano in Japan. Kilimanjaro rises high above the African plains. The highest mountain in the United States is Mount McKinley in Alaska. Its snowy top is a little less than five miles high.

# FAMOUS MOUNTAINS OF THE BIBLE

*Come, let us go up to the mountain of the Lord.* Micah 4:2

***Top*** **Some people think that this mountain, Jabal al Lawz, is the place called Mount Sinai where Moses received the Ten Commandments. No one knows for sure where the real Mount Sinai is.**

***Bottom*** **One of the most famous mountains of the Bible is Mount Ararat, where Noah's ark came to rest.**

Many people believe that gods live in the high places of mountains. We know that the real God does not live on mountains. His creation is separate from Him. Instead, He has used mountains in special ways. In fact, one of God's names is *El Shaddai,* which in Hebrew means, "the One as mighty as a mountain."

Many important things happened on mountains in the Bible. Ezekiel called the Garden of Eden "the holy mount of God" (Ezekiel 28:14). God made His covenant, or promise, with Abraham on Mount Moriah (Genesis 22), and Jesus gave his "Sermon on the Mount" (Matthew 5-7) on a mountain. And it was on Mount Sinai that Moses saw the burning bush. The Bible tells us what the mountain looked like: "Mount Sinai was wrapped in smoke, because the LORD descended on it in fire. And the smoke of it went up like the smoke of a kiln, and the whole mountain quaked greatly." (Exodus 19:18) On Mount Sinai the Lord gave Moses the Ten Commandments which help us to live a godly life.

Another very special mountain is Mount Ararat. Like Mount Sinai, Mount Ararat is a volcano. It rises out of the plains of Turkey like a gigantic ice cream cone. The Bible tells

Moses must have seen wonderful and terrifying things when he went up to the top of Mount Sinai to meet with God.

us that Noah's ark, filled with the animals of the world, "came to rest on the moutains of Ararat" (Genesis 8:4). Noah's ark was huge, as long as thirty cars! Although it was built thousands of years ago, the cold of Mt. Ararat may have saved it beneath ice and snow. People have tried to find it, but nobody has for sure . . . yet. Perhaps someday you will climb the mountain and see what Noah's ark was really like!

*Inset* **These rocks have been twisted and broken by strong forces within the Earth.**

**How do fossils get to the tops of mountains? Were they brought there by the flood mentioned in the Bible, or were they pushed up from ancient seas by the forces God put inside the Earth?**

# How Old Are the Mountains?

**Everywhere on Earth we find layers of rock, like we see in Bryce Canyon.**

*As a mountain erodes and crumbles and as a rock is moved from its place, as water wears away stones and torrents wash away the soil . . .*
Job 14:18

Mountains have been around since the beginning of the Earth. We have already seen how some mountains are made. But mountains are full of mystery, and one of the greatest mysteries is just how old they are.

When we look at the side of a mountain, we see many layers of rock and dirt. The layers are different colors. Within these layers we find *fossils*. Fossils are skeletons of dead animals from long ago that have become hard as stone after many years. We even find fossils of old fish on the very tops of mountains!

Some people think the fossils in high places were carried there by the Flood mentioned in the Bible. The Book of Genesis tells us that this great flood covered the entire Earth. The flood waters also may have laid down the layers of rock in the mountains. Other people think that the fossils used to live in oceans that dried up long ago. The fossils were pushed up as the Earth's plates turned the ocean bottom into mountains. The mountains might be older than the Flood in the Bible. Maybe there are other reasons the mountains look the way they do. What do you think?

No matter how the mountains formed, and no matter how long they have been around, mountains were created by God.

# GOD'S PEOPLE IN THE MOUNTAINS

*Above* **The hill country of Canaan protected God's people.**

*Right* **It was on mountaintops where many important things in the Bible happened.**

*As the mountains surround Jerusalem, so the Lord surrounds his people both now and forevermore.* Psalm 125:2

Mountains have been a big part of God's plans all along. After the people of Israel had wandered in the desert for forty years, God brought them to the Promised Land. This place was mostly in the high mountains overlooking the desert. It was a cool place with hills and valleys and lots of water. Grapes and olive trees grew there, and they called it a "land of milk and honey." Since the Promised Land was in the mountains, no war chariots could come attack the Israelites, and they were safe from enemies. God took care of His children by leading them into the mountains.

In the New Testament, Jesus was born on a small mountain in the city of Bethlehem. Bethlehem is on a high hill near Jerusalem. Later, Jesus was given a test high on another mountain. Satan showed Him the kingdoms of the world from the mountain peak, and said to Him, "All this I will give you . . . if you will bow down and worship me" (Matthew 4:9). But Jesus said to Satan, just as He says to us today, "Worship the Lord your God, and serve him only" (Matthew 4:10). Perhaps this is the best lesson we can learn from the mountains.

# GLACIERS AND ICEBERGS

*The mountains melt beneath him and the valleys split apart,
like wax before the fire, like water rushing down a slope.* Micah 1:4

What moves more slowly than molasses, is colder than ice cream, and can carry whole pieces of mountains or carve valleys through solid rock? The answer is, a *glacier.* Glaciers are rivers of solid ice. Most are as far across as many football fields, and some are hundreds of miles long.

A glacier begins as a field of ice high in the mountains. As snow falls on top of the ice each year, it becomes packed very tightly. Finally, the field of ice becomes so heavy that it begins to creep down the mountain, helped along by a thin layer of water in the ground beneath it. As the glacier moves down the mountain, it carries with it boulders and rocks from the high country. Rocks under the ice grind deep gouges in the rock below and polish it to a beautiful shine. After many years a glacier can scrape out entire valleys. Some people call glaciers "God's polishing tools."

Glaciers sometimes end in a lake or ocean. In the water, giant chunks of ice break off to become floating ice mountains called *icebergs.* Only the top of an iceberg sticks out of the water. Ships must stay far away from icebergs so they don't run into the part hidden under the water. The famous ship *Titanic* sank after accidentally running into an iceberg.

**The gigantic oceanliner *R.M.S. Titanic* was thought to be unsinkable. It struck an iceberg that tore through the belly of the ship. Many people died because there were not enough lifeboats.**

***Right*** **This beautiful iceberg floats away from the Bering Glacier on a calm sea.**

*Inset top* Icebergs in the Gulf of Alaska can be a danger to ships.

*Inset middle* The Bering Glacier is a swirl of ice that slowly pours into the Gulf of Alaska, breaking into thousands of icebergs.

*Inset bottom* Crevasse in glacier: Dangerous cracks, called *crevasses,* can be hidden under a crust of ice and snow on glaciers. This glacier is in Iceland.

# CRATERS

*The second angel sounded his trumpet, and something like a huge mountain, all ablaze, was thrown into the sea.* Revelation 8:8a

A *crater* is a giant bowl-shaped place in the ground. Volcanoes usually have craters on the very top where the lava and ash come out. Some craters are on flat ground around geysers. There is a giant crater in Death Valley, California, that is two-thirds of a mile across! It was made when a volcano exploded under the ground. The crater is called *Ubehebe,* which is a Shoshone Indian word meaning "basket." It is a very big basket!

Some craters are not made by volcanoes. There are craters on most of the moons and many planets that were caused by flying rocks called *meteors.* Meteors are like mountains of rock that float through space. When one smashes into a planet or moon, it makes a big hole, or crater. The Earth has many such craters, though not as many as some places. Our air protects us from meteors, and the Earth's

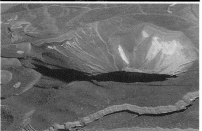

*Top* **This crater was made by a meteor that fell from space. Scientists think the meteor was the size of a railroad car!**

*Middle, bottom* **Volcanic crater in Death Valley: This crater in Death Valley, California, was made by a volcanic explosion.**

weather erases the old craters. The Moon is covered with craters. Since the Moon has so many craters, what do you think is different about the Moon and the Earth?

One big crater on Earth is called the Meteor Crater, in Arizona. You can find another crater on a map of Canada. If you look carefully at a place called Hudson Bay, you will see that part of it is round. It is a very old crater, filled with the ocean. There are other meteor craters in Australia, in Africa, and on all the continents of the world.

In 1978, a meteor exploded over Chicago. It was so far up in the sky
that nobody saw it, but the event was noticed by a spy satellite.

# CANYONS

*Every valley shall be raised up, every mountain and hill made low . . .*
Isaiah 40:4

Our world has many wonderful high places, but it has low places, too. Sometimes the plates of the Earth pull away from each other, or rivers cut through valleys and wash away the soil, and a *canyon* is made. A canyon is a deep valley with steep sides.

The biggest canyon in the world is the Great Rift Valley in Africa. It begins as a gentle valley by the Jordan River, a place where many Bible people have lived. The valley goes all the way down through the Red Sea and into Africa, where it gets much bigger. It doesn't end until it gets almost to the end of Africa. Standing on the edge of the Great Rift Valley feels like standing on the edge of forever. It is often filled with clouds and looks like a cliff falling into the sky below. But under those clouds, it is a very beautiful place with giraffes, elephants, zebras and other animals. This canyon was probably caused by the shifting of two plates.

***Thingvullir*** **is a canyon in Iceland that is being pulled apart about three centimeters every hundred years. The shifting of the Earth's plates is the force which is making the canyon wider.**

Another beautiful canyon is the Grand Canyon in Arizona. It is a rocky place with a river winding through the bottom. It is more than 200 miles long, and in some places it is a mile deep! Some scientists think the Grand Canyon was carved out by the Colorado River that is now in the bottom of the canyon. Others say a great flood like the one described in the Bible created it very quickly. Its sides are covered in thousands of thin, colorful layers of rock.

**Great floods have changed the face of our Earth, cutting deep canyons and valleys across the landscape.**

***Insets*** **Arches National Monument. Goblin Valley. Moab. Water and wind have sculpted these three places into deep canyons and strange forms.**

# EARTHQUAKES

*Then there came . . . a severe earthquake . . . The great city split into three parts, and the cities of the nations collapsed.*  Revelation 16:18-19

As long as people have lived on God's Earth, there have been earthquakes. The ground seems to be nice and hard, but underneath, there is a lot going on! Underground rivers gurgle through the rocks, and boulders shift back and forth between each other. Magma rumbles through rock tunnels far beneath our feet. This is the way our world was designed. But sometimes the shifting rocks way down there shake us up way up here!

An *earthquake* is like a wave rolling through the rocks. Just like in a lake or ocean, some waves are small, and some are big. Most are very small, and nobody feels them. But every once in a while, in certain places in the world, earthquakes can be very strong. The ground shakes and rumbles, windows break, streets crack, and sometimes whole buildings fall to the ground.

Many places in the world have never felt earthquakes. But in California, in Mexico, Japan, in parts of Russia and China, and on many islands, earthquakes are dangerous. In a place called Kobe, Japan, an earthquake turned an entire highway upside-down! Many people were hurt or killed.

God sometimes uses earthquakes to help people or to cause change. The Book of Revelation tells of a great earthquake that destroys evil. Paul and Silas were singing praises to God when an earthquake broke their prison open (Acts 16)!

God also uses earthquakes to show His power. A violent earthquake shook Jerusalem when Jesus was crucified (Matthew 27), and another came with an angel to announce Jesus' resurrection (Matthew 28).

A terrible earthquake rumbled through the city of Kobe in Japan. It turned this highway on its side and destroyed entire buildings.

*Inset* The book of Revelation describes an earthquake that God uses to destroy an evil city called Babylon. This picture shows Babylon as a great temple that is being split in half.

# Volcanoes and Earthquakes in Other Places

*Inset* The winding mountains of Ganymede might look like this up close. Here we can see the icy mountains that have been shoved up by forces under the ground.

Jupiter's moon Ganymede shows signs of twisted mountains and canyons much like some places on Earth

*On that day . . . the Mount of Olives will be split in two from east to west, forming a great valley, with half of the mountain moving north and half moving south.* Zechariah 14:4

The Earth is not the only one of God's worlds with volcanoes. We have seen huge volcanoes on Venus, on Mars, and on many moons. Most of the volcanoes we have found on other worlds have been dead for a very long time. But our spacecraft have actually snapped photos of volcanoes erupting on Jupiter's moon, Io, and on Neptune's moon, Triton. Some scientists think the volcanoes of Venus may still be active. And we know that where there are volcanoes there are also earthquakes.

We have also seen mountains that have been stretched and pulled just like Earth's mountains. One such place is Jupiter's planet-sized moon, Ganymede. Ganymede has long ridges which have slipped just like the plates on Earth. Sometimes these plates have split mountains or craters in half, moving one side up and the other side down!

So, while God builds His mountains and canyons here on Earth, He is building others on the planets and moons, too! God's power is all around us, even far beyond the Earth.

Sometimes we feel like things in our lives are hard. It is as if we must climb a mountain that is too steep, or as if everything is all shaken up. But no matter what kind of "earthquakes" or "volcanoes" we have in our life, or what kind of mountains we must climb, God will be there to help us. He reminds us of that each time we look at His wonderful mountains, His volcanoes, and His power beneath our feet.

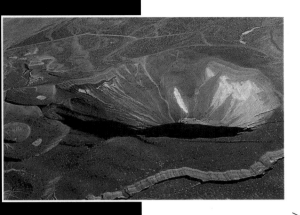

# Glossary

**atoms** (Ah-tumz): tiny building blocks that combine together to make everything in the universe.

**canyon** (CAN-yun): a deep valley with steep sides.

**crater** (KRAY-ter): a large bowl-shaped pit in the ground, made by volcanoes or meteors.

**eruption** (ee-RUP-shun): when a volcano spits out lava, rock, and ash.

**fossil** (FOS-il): a dead animal that has turned to stone after many years.

**geyser** (GUY-zur): a hot stream of water that shoots out of the ground.